WHAT'S MISSING IN YOUR

JOB SEARCH

BY SCOTT GARDNER

DEDICATION

Throughout our work lives others we meet help shape the way we think about business, people, or both. Their keen understanding of business, systems, processes, and people allow them to make contributions that grow their company's business. They also help all to develop and grow as employees and as individuals. Their tact, diplomacy, style, and grace (often under fire) help each of us to achieve the goal of strong career satisfaction.

While no one deserves more credit for their support of my career than my wife and confidant Teri and my son Scott, I also have to say thank you to my parents and two sisters (Leslie and Linda). I'd also like to call out just a few business and human resources people who supported my professional development within Human Resources: Ivan Dryer, Bob Spitz, Mike Miller, Jay Colvin, Al Bormann, Frank Chabre, Tom Sumrall, Don Black, John Fleischer, Jim Osment, Jim Franklin, Ian Ziskin, Janice Waterman, Carolyn Biggs-Harris, Philip Alford, Gilles Godin, Allan Toomer, Andrea Roschke, Ron Burr, Betty Boyiazis, Chuck Best, Alice Cheung, Chuck Harris, Jody Barry, Eric Lane, Jody L'Esperance and Kristina Mclaughlan. In the special thanks group for their continuing friendship and support: Kurtis Kishi, Jim Renteria, John Arany, Jeri Gerner, Anita Baxter, Kay Case, Vicki Morris, Karen Togno, Larry Fetty, John Faulkner, Don Lewis, Meredith Gendell-Rosen, Nader Nasseh,

Steve Hoofring, Sharat Shankar, Jack Wilson, Eric Lookhoff, and Thomas Wu. Taylor Gardner, thank you for the book photo.

Family members and friends help us to find a balance outside of work. They keep us centered and focused on other aspects of life. They remind us where we came from and where we are today, and even of where we said we were headed. They might share their thoughts of where they think we really are headed.

These two very different groups of people have helped me to look back on my career choices and they make me feel good about my contributions in Human Resources. While I can trace my inner peace and happiness with my life's work to many experiences in and out of work, I am thankful to so many people for being a large part of my career and making it what it has been. Many of these relationships continue to grow today, and for that I'm eternally grateful. I value those relationships more than any of my work accomplishments.

There were also many other special friends, co-workers, and extended family members who were fully supportive all along the way and to all of them I say thank you.

PREFACE

My purpose here is to combine many experiences from my career in Human Resources into a guide for improving a job candidate's search capabilities and likelihood for being hired. This book is different; it covers not only the technical aspects of conducting the job search, but makes suggestions as to the metamorphosis that you individually may need to undergo to both improve your likelihood for being offered a position with each interview you complete and then helping you to find greater job satisfaction and perhaps gain new recognition in the workplace. While this may seem like a large undertaking, I believe that once you understand some key elements of job search, how you may be evaluated and critiqued throughout the course of your interviews, you can achieve not just employment, but meaningful employment.

This material will include opinions/biases based on my years of HR experience, my interpretation of articles, books, and suggestions made by others, and, what I've seen work or not work for people searching for jobs at all levels of the job pyramid both before and after 2008.

Let me call out the first section on education to put some of the early discussed material in its proper context. Because this opening section addresses high school, early career planning, the GED, exploring advanced education, and covers the topic of military service, all of the material in this section may or may not be relevant to you and your life today. My intent is to share with you the importance I've placed on education, planning, and the development of a job search strategy that can be successful for you. Regardless of your current level of education and where you find yourself in the career planning stage, by books-end, I believe you will find material important to you and a necessary part of your toolbox.

As an HR professional, I experienced many different on the job situations-the kind that shape the way we think and feel about others. I have interviewed, supported, and managed small- and large-scale recruitment hiring efforts that brought new life to my employer when times were good. At the other extreme, there were also times of employer struggle, where I participated in or managed small layoffs (where as few as one or two people were impacted) on up to much larger efforts, where as many as three or four hundred people were laid off at a time.

Looking back over a career that extended well over thirty years, I can remember the hires of executives, individual contributors, and team players who would go on to make solid contributions for my employer and who were rewarded. But, I also remember the many employees, up and down the pay scale, who, through no real fault of their own, found their way to the unemployment line because my employer determined that a cutback in people was the next crucial step in their business cycle. After years of managing or overseeing this revolving door, I began to capture my thoughts along the way and vowed to get them down on paper in the hope that someone might benefit from what I was learning.

Presently, more people worldwide find themselves without jobs and for some, they clearly see no opportunities. There are few valuable resources available to help them through job search and/or to better their situation where they are employed. Often the unemployed are told - by their inner selves, those close to them, or by the media- that they have to keep reaching out and to keep going. However, those comments often come without practical suggestions for action. This fact prompted me to write this book to get you to think about your work or life situation now before another day passes and an employment opportunity goes unanswered. If I can get you to look closely at yourself, perhaps you will change certain behaviors, if necessary, and your approaches to your current employer (if you have one) or to the job market that hinders or even prevents you from achieving a greater level of job and career satisfaction.

While I haven't seen everything in the workplace, I do know that I've lived through, and witnessed more than many of you have because of my organizational role in corporate America. Some of what you will read and think about will certainly not be new, or even revolutionary, but maybe, just maybe, I'm getting to you at a time in your life where you will listen to suggestions and take actions to correct behaviors, in and out of the workplace, that may be undermining your successes. Perhaps all you need to do to improve your chances for career success (including increased longevity with your employer, if that is what you want) is to change how you look and how you verbalize around problem-solving. More specifically, I mean learning that you should communicate findings and solutions so that others see you as knowledgeable, a team player, company loyalist, and valuable to the company's future success. Such sharing may then lead you to find clues or tips that will help you to find greater job and personal satisfaction.

Key Point: Keep in mind at all times that effective communication is at the core of any job search and any role you successfully fill within a company. Most often your style, approach to communication, and, your ability to convey thoughts and ideas trigger responses in others that either opens or closes the doors of opportunity. Communication needs to convey understanding and knowledge of the work involved, confidence that you can either lead or be part of a team that can complete it, and that your every waking effort is to make your leaders and your company successful. If the quality of our communication matches or exceeds the high quality of work we perform, we often find a new and greater level of job satisfaction and reward.

In the current economic climate where we see companies come and go like no other time in our country's history, you simply cannot measure personal/career success or self worth simply by longevity with a particular employer. Rather, you must find an inner peace with your work performance (and output) past and present regardless of where you work as that may be all you feel you have to show for your efforts at the end of your career or employment with one company. Regardless of a company's lifespan or our employment with a given company, what I've learned is that we each must strive to build a today and tomorrow for ourselves.

In this book, I hope you find thoughts and ideas that can work for you as you seek both success and opportunity in your work career.

Scott R Gardner

TABLE OF CONTENTS

CHAPTER 1:
Education And Career Planning

Whether people want to believe it or not, planning and preparation for the job search begins at a very early age, with both our upbringing and personal thoughts around the importance of education. While some struggle to find time and interest in education, others pursue learning and education throughout their lives.

I grew up in a household where it was impressed upon me early that learning was life-long and I was destined to attend college because Mom and Dad stated there were no other options. As I look back, I'm very thankful for that.

I have indelible memories of how I learned the importance of education. A time or two (or three), Dad sat me in front of a chalkboard at home and worked with me on algebra, geometry, and English composition. While I barely passed the math classes (certainly fared better in English), those memories stand out as moments with my Dad that demonstrated the importance he found in learning. I certainly appreciate the emphasis he placed on my education.

We took the same approach to education that my parents impressed upon me with our son, Scott. He was never allowed to think that he wouldn't be going on to college; in fact, he worked harder in college than he had in high school and fared even better academically by the time he graduated.

For me (and, I think, for many of those that I grew up around), schooling beyond high school taught me how to take a more balanced approach to both life and career, instilling in me a certain kind of logic and reasoning that my high school didn't teach-and one I suspect many will not learn coming out of high school but then have to learn in the workplace. Call it what you will, but I believe the classes and instructors at this advanced level help us to develop thoughts, views, and opinions that most high school teachers can only explore with their students (at a surface level) given the demands placed upon them by both the curriculum and the school administration.

Generally speaking, most agree that college graduates have a greater opportunity (and therefore greater likelihood) to succeed than nongrads. Of course, there are exceptions to this rule; perhaps you are one of them. But, while I believe that choosing to work full time after high school versus the pursuit of advanced learning can teach you important life skills, the overwhelming majority of current businesses view education at a young adult age (with the years from eighteen to twenty-five) to be more valuable than work experience when determining pay and opportunity. Teri and I believed that Scott's advanced education was necessary for him to have more opportunities and choices in job selection. He would likely make more money earlier in his career as well. We believed that bringing the college diploma to the interview table would open more doors for Scott than his high school diploma and we were all about getting doors opened for him.

Though my discussions with my dad about schooling ended (I went!), my lessons in communication and relationship building did not. While Dad and I sometimes struggled in our verbal communication with each other; all our interactions helped me learn the importance of the human relationship. I also learned that no matter how smart, bright, energetic, ambitious and driven you are, there will come a point in your personal development or in your business that you must depend on the will and skills of others. You'll have to rely on someone else, sometime.

The ability to communicate is at the core of every successful business person and everyone who desires loving working relationships. You may learn to communicate through interactions with a family member or another close contact. You may learn it as a very small child (if you are fortunate), or much, much later in life.

CHAPTER 2:
High School Diploma/GED

Let me start this section by saying that I believe everyone in this country is entitled to an education and that everyone should strive to achieve a high school diploma. It is a right you have as a citizen of this country. While I understand that some peoples' situations may make it difficult, they need to set their sights on a diploma nonetheless. Where attending a high school program may be too large an obstacle to overcome, the GED (General Educational Development) testing program may be another option. I'd encourage you to figure out how you are either going to get the diploma or how you will pass the GED through any legal means necessary. Job opportunities for those with at least a high school diploma or equivalent always seem to be greater than for those without. Statistical reports continue to show those with a high school diploma will fare better than those with no diploma in the job search process.

Once they get a High School Diploma, it was all too common to hear some people say, "No additional education required for me. I am ready to go out, get a job, and get paid". They would then spend a year (or two or three or more) on the job and then find themselves asking, "Why is this person, with less work experience (but more schooling) than me, being considered for the better-paying job? That, is the job that I should be filling."

As the senior HR person for many of the companies that typically employed those with skills in manufacturing, assembly, lower-level administration, clerical support, and/or customer support, the number of people I've heard say this over the course of more than thirty years would easily run into the hundreds. Nearly every single one of them had a reason for why their education stopped at high school. And do you know what? In nearly every case, it was not because of anything other than the desire or need to get a paycheck rather than get schooling.

You want my take on this? If a paycheck is all you desire out of your life's work then a paycheck is the most you will ever find in it. In that case, work will never satisfy you, and somehow, something will find a way to keep you below your full pay potential. You need to embark on a plan of continuous learning through courses and/or practical training programs.

CHAPTER 3:
Advanced Education

I have to be honest and admit that there are people who have simply "made it" without formalized schooling beyond high school, but they are the exception and not the rule. While not everyone is cut out for two or four-year college, trade school or military service, my message to you is that this is an important time in your life. Decisions you make at this stage can often times have an enormous effect on what your options, choices, and decisions are later on. I'd ask you to keep in mind that often those later decisions impact more than just yourself. They often impact a spouse, significant other, or one or more other family members (all too often, children). Declining the next level of schooling, advanced education, trade skills training, or military service for a paycheck because you just "want a break" from school or you don't think you need to do anything other than make money now is all too often a short sighted decision made in youth. My experience tells me that the same people often make quick personal choices without full reasoning that often lead to poorly timed lifestyle choices,(i.e., increased debt, taking on family responsibilities when they aren't emotionally or financially prepared, and so on). As we have seen over and over again, decisions like these made without proper regard for the possible consequences are much more difficult to change a few years down the road and often with far greater consequences to you (and everyone around you).

Given the number of people that I've listened to, counseled, guided, and watched over the years, I've never really understood why so many people simply buckle under pressure. Many of them do nothing constructive to improve their situations; they usually turn away from solutions that require time and effort (i.e., seeking greater education and training). Most will settle for the status quo without as much as a whimper for something better for themselves. They truly don't see that this type of decision stays with them for a lifetime until months or years have passed. Some truly never really think about it again and that truly stumps me.

All too often people make short-sighted decisions and simply take what they can get at the time. They don't plan; they don't think out how short or long their lives are actually going to be. I suggest you adopt this strategy and philosophical approach to life:

1) Plan and make decisions that have **both** the best short-term and long-term impact.

2) Don't just live your life day-to-day; rather have an action plan for tomorrow-and the day after, because you may still need a life to live here (on earth). Unless something throws you a curveball and cuts your life short, you will be here tomorrow and the next day. Your day-to-day philosophy and strategy may then not get you through the other pitches (my baseball analogy here---slider, knuckleball, fastball, etc.) that life will eventually throw at you. Not knowing how to handle each pitch will make your comeback more difficult to achieve.

3) Make planning and preparation as interesting and exciting as the outcome, because it, too, is all part of the journey.

4) Career planning is like baking a cake or preparing for your big concert or game performance. The preparation makes the victories that much more exciting. The losses we each suffer along the way are easier to turn into wins when we apply what we learn from them to the next big event.

The decision to go on with your education is not the last one you need to make. You then must decide what your education will focus on. What do you want to learn? And, what do you need to learn? Look at what you know and are learning every day. What interests, education and experience would give you the best opportunity to apply your new skills in the workplace? Advanced education is often very expensive so you should aim for a good return on investment before you take on the expense. To simply major in a subject that offers little to no employment potential is simply a bad financial decision and could result in debt for all of your adult life. Look at all the people out there who have enormous school debt and little hope for no jobs in their chosen fields. While I don't think it is a rational argument to say that you're going to work immediately after high school because of all the college debt you hear about, I do think considerable thought and planning are needed before you take on debt of any kind without a truly workable plan to get it all paid back.

While advanced education may increase the likelihood for your career success, rational and sound business decisions will help determine-and certainly have some impact on-your level of happiness. Simply educating yourself without an implementation plan is not a recipe for success. As for everything else discussed in this book, you need a rational plan. Life is like any movie or TV show; there has to be script or plan to follow if you want people to follow along with you. Unscripted lives like unscripted shows don't often bring the happiness and security most of us seek. When we stop learning and settle in to a plan of "just being ok" and not seeking new challenges, it is not uncommon for us to see dramatic lifestyle changes which may impact the types of people we attract, fewer job opportunities we might have once sought coming our direction, and a complacency that didn't exist when our life journey started.

Let's look at some things you can plan for best results. While you pursue a diploma or certificate in a specific major or skill area, your activities outside of the classroom should reflect a professional interest in your chosen field. Whenever possible this means accepting a co-op role, an internship, or part-time or summer work that has some relationship to what you wish to do once you have your diploma or certificate. In this economy and job market, I'd encourage a student to aim for an outside job that offers experience relevant to future work rather than one that might pay better in the present but has no direct relationship at all. While I understand that many students have bills to pay or need savings to support their education, my advice is based on my belief that if all else is equal, companies more often select graduates whose outside work is closest to their own before those with unrelated work experience. (On the other hand, doing nothing is not an option you should consider!)

To implement your plan, you should not only research schools and majors, but also visit or contact the career planning and placement office of the school you choose. Ask:

1) What prominent businesses does the college/university have relationships with?

2) Is the purpose of these relationships to identify prospective student interns? If so, how may I find out when those opportunities are available?

3) Could you please provide me with a list of companies that recruit on campus via on-site interviews and job fairs.

4) Are there opportunities for me to meet company representatives when they visit the campus?

5) How can I obtain a schedule of school-year events coordinated through this office?

6) What interviewing and hiring data can I obtain through the school?

7) Are there any prominent alumni that you might suggest I contact for job opportunities?

8) Should nothing in industry be available, are there student work opportunities within the placement office?

9) How do I schedule an appointment with my school's career counselor?

Your research here will help you to determine whether you begin your search for relevant work experience in your freshman or sophomore year. Your search for full-time work should begin **at least** six months prior to graduation date.

During the 1980s, I was first a recruiter and then a manager of one of the nation's largest and most prominent college recruiting programs. On average, my employer would hire in excess of a thousand new college undergraduates and graduates every year. Our program covered many of the nation's engineering, computer science and business schools from Hawaii to Puerto Rico. For weeks at a time, recruiters would invade the selected campuses and interview anywhere from twelve to fifteen students per day to help sustain and build our various businesses. Students were selected for a variety of different reasons, including major, GPA (grade point average) within their major and overall, communication skills, subject matter (elective courses within their major), and presentation skills. Students who had the foresight to gain outside work experience and maintain a good GPA were often in the top tier of consideration.

While the general state of the economy, or even local business economics, will determine the job market and the opportunities available for students, you still have the power to determine how you spend your time outside the classroom. Should relevant work experience not be available, then look for ways to expand your growth and learning. Perhaps you could volunteer or do community work on or near campus, tutor, or take part-time work that is unrelated to your future career. The point here is that you are never "just" a full time student; you are committed to your future and to making a real contribution to any employer.

Although work assignments are more difficult to find today than they were in the Seventies and Eighties, the emphasis on hiring well-rounded candidates has not changed. Employers want versatility in their employees, and they want to believe that each and every one will contribute to the goals and aspirations of the company. I believe that this is truer today than it has ever been since I graduated from college in the mid-seventies.

CHAPTER 4:
Military Service

While I truly honor those of you who select military service after high school or as a career, you must still make some choices; what trade or marketable skills do you wish to learn? What skills do you wish to have when you leave the military?

Many veterans leave the service without a clear plan or path for entering the workforce. Many return to school but are often still uncertain about why and about what they want out of it. You need a plan of action and a focus beyond your enlistment period. Perhaps you consider enlistment to be simply a commitment of so many years of your life, the same way someone else may look at a potential employer. Perhaps you consider military service a career. Regardless of your level of commitment, you need to set goals that meet your career aspirations and your chosen lifestyle.

Military service offers you short or long term commitment options; you may not have decided on a long-term plan when you enlist, but it is important that both your short and long term goals get equal time in your career planning when you discuss opportunities with an armed forces recruitment officer. Whether you've decided on a four year commitment or one of twenty or more years, it is highly likely that your working career will not end when your military service does. In other words, your thought process about the skills you want and need to learn cannot wait until your military service ends. You simply cannot put off the planning.

Military service provides a variety of training types. Leadership in the military does not always translate into leadership in private industry unless your specific job skills are very relevant. You need to plan to acquire skills in the service that directly translate to private industry; these are so-called "transferable" skills. Unfortunately, many in the military overlook this point. Without "transferable" skills, industry will likely not credit you as one who has obtained the specific skills they seek to perform the job the company is looking to fill. In essence, you will likely lose any edge you could have obtained from your military role because the necessary skills to perform the role in the private sector cannot be clearly demonstrated.

I'd encourage veterans to research programs offered through the federal government, such as the Veterans Retraining Assistance Program (VRAP). Check the federal or state employment programs listed on the United States Department of Labor website. Perhaps a program such as TurboTAP.org (listed on the Department of Defense website) could be of benefit to you.

Regardless of your education and experience, you will eventually make the decision to enter the workplace and seek employment in some capacity. Your job search can be focused on local businesses that serve our communities or you may decide to expand your job search to nationwide or even global sized companies.

Please explore all the Internet sites available to you as a veteran to assist you in your job search. At the time this book was being published, numerous companies throughout the U.S. have advertised their job openings in an effort to attract veterans. I encourage all veterans to both identify and apply for those job openings. As the saying goes, leave no stone unturned, especially as it relates to your job search.

CHAPTER 5:
Job Search Preparation

For at least five years now, we have all had to learn to maneuver our way through the struggling economic climate where thousands upon thousands of jobs have gone away, likely never to come back. While you may or may not be successful to date in your job search efforts, you likely have learned many painstaking lessons that you'd not like to repeat, or have others experience if they can learn from you.

It is in troubled and scary financial times, that we sometimes follow our own bad advice or the advice of those not familiar with today's job search environment and lose valuable time and energy in our job search. This often leads to no job and no foreseeable job opportunities. Fortunately, even in this economy, you can find those successful job searchers who have learned their lessons well and from whom we can learn from. Much of what you will get here comes from those many people with whom I've met over these many years.

Let's compare, for example, the decline in the aerospace industry in the late eighties and early nineties with the recent NASA cutbacks of the past few years. The moving trucks are literally backing up to the door of these businesses and telling employees in big, bold letters, "Hey! There is little to no work coming in here. You need to find another place to work."

Yet, the reaction from many (maybe most) was something like "I'm going to put my head down and pretend like this really isn't going to happen. It certainly won't happen to me, and even if it did, where would I go to make this kind of money? I like the work here! There is no way that NASA will undergo such a drastic change."

My response? WOW.....I guess they did!

In February 1995, the Los Angeles Times printed an article quoting me (and others) on the current state of the local employment marketplace on the front page of the Valley business section. Like today, at that time many were unemployed, or on the verge of it, because the aerospace and defense industry were in a downslide. Defense contractors and their suppliers were all feeling the pinch of tightened federal budgets and a rescaling of the industry. The article was about how many people would need to go to smaller, less government driven companies (many of whom also paid less), since many of the larger, mainstay companies were not hiring.

The article was accompanied by a photo of me sitting at my work desk, hidden behind stacks of resumes that my staff and I had collected as a result of recent recruitment ads. Many of those resumes were from laid-off aerospace workers who simply had not believed they would be fired. Many did not see or heed the warning signals and had stayed too long; many were now shocked at the pay they were offering. Many held out, waiting for the world to change. It didn't. They lost valuable time by not finding work or learning new skills. Simply put, many of their current skills were not relevant to our specific business, our pay ranges did not support their requested level of compensation, and they expected my company to support a standard of living they had grown accustomed to. They felt they were entitled to what they had earned over the years. "Where does it say that the world owes anyone a living, or that any company is bound to make one's life whole?"

The world has changed. If you are laid off or terminated, you will be lucky to get what you once earned. Industry is more likely to value you if you are currently employed when you change jobs, and, you might get the same or better compensation (although there are no guarantees). Call it wrong, call it circumstantial, and call it whatever you want-but this is the way it is right now.

I want you to find a job-one that is, better paying and more satisfying, but you simply will not get there by dreaming about getting something that you have no control over. You must create opportunities for yourself and master the skills necessary to make it happen. I will never tell you to give up, but you need to understand that this work is hard and may challenge you to a <u>new</u> degree. It will require your full effort and concentration. Countless times I've seen people who were fired suddenly sit back, retreat from society, and grow angry, unhappy, upset, or frustrated because of their most recent employment experience. The bottom line is, you cannot do that in this economy. You must immediately pick yourself up and begin the job search process. Each day, week, month, or year you sit without working will work against you when you seek a new job. Look at part-time jobs, internships, charity, and volunteer work in all industries while you seek full-time work. You must stay connected to the workforce to maximize your job search efforts!

I've often been asked when the job search process should begin. My answer is usually "**Now**". This is true whether you are unemployed, under-employed, or unhappy in a current job (or if your instincts tell you that something is going at your place of employment that might impact your current job). Just because you have a job, you are not necessarily secure.

Of course, if you've been let go (you might even feel you were blind-sided), begin your job search immediately.

One of the clear learnings that successful job searchers have shared is that allowing your job search to go both unmanaged and uncontrolled allows the job search to take a life of its own. What happens then is that the search can, in fact, become both harmful to your projected image to employers (given its lack of attention or focus to a specific type of job opening) and to your own health (often leading to feelings of depression and lack of self-worth). As most often happens, the shotgun approach to the job search process (where resumes are scattered across multiple companies in a geographic space for a multitude of different types of jobs) can be both time-wasting and expensive at a time when in the early days of a job loss an effective strategy is most needed. Bottom-line, an undisciplined job search (with no opportunity for hiring via referral) is likely to be unsuccessful at finding you a job. A good job search (whether you start it on Day One or simply want to re-start it today) requires a plan, strategy and timetable.

While the plan includes all elements of the job search process, the strategy is how we will implement the plan each and every day. You must decide upon a strategy for how people are going to learn about you as you seek job opportunities. There should be an on-going effort to identify potential employers as well as key personal contacts who can forward your resume to hiring managers. Be prepared to use any and all strategies to get your name out to potential employers. You can use walk-ins; postal mail; e-mail; deliver communications through family, friends, or acquaintances; phone; on-line chat; and so on. Your strategy can be flexible; your goal is simply to get a job interview.

We then need to develop a timetable with days and dates that clearly outlines when tasks are to be completed. Any job search comes with a multiple number of tasks to be completed so you need to create a timetable. This timetable should include the specific date of a ready-to-go resume, specific dates specific company research should be completed, record cover letters and resumes submitted, interviews scheduled, etc. Without a timetable for quickly completing the preliminary tasks, you may miss opportunities, and you don't want that. You may decide later that a given opportunity (job offer) is not what you want, but for now, you do not want to miss out on any of them.

Resume preparation is the critical element in any job search. People often just don't understand that a resume document is a written representation of a job seeker. It's a document that opens a window into who we are and allows others to see into some piece of our life's journey. What can be more important than that? **I liken the finished resume product to a movie experience-----if I don't like the preview, I doubt I'll see the movie!**

Often times, people would tell me in the early stages of their job search that they believed the job search would be simple because they sought jobs in the same field (assuming those jobs still exist). They would say, "When they see my level of experience, I'll be hired quickly. Look at how my resume emphasizes the experience." Many did not seem to get that many of the jobs being eliminated were jobs requiring similar experience, and, even if you found companies hiring for your particular experience, the effort required to be hired for the job was often substantially more difficult than the job search effort being put towards it. Why? Because of fewer jobs, many more similarly qualified people were now competing for those fewer jobs.

There is also another element to today's job market. You need to be prepared to not only compete for a job against others who may have the same, or more experience in your area of expertise, but possibly be ready to compete for this job against any and all other experienced applicants who will inundate employers with their resumes.

Why should all this be of concern?

Because you simply don't know the thought process behind the company creating this job opening. While the posting may reflect many of the specific skills and experiences the company seeks, the posting will not share the qualities and attributes the company seeks to find in the individual they plan to hire.

The job search process has also evolved in another way: it is now very technology based. If you have been with one company for so many years that this technological change has passed right by you, and you now find yourself seeking new employment, you will need to understand what has changed and how you need to work differently this time around.

Desktop computers are now being replaced by laptops, tablets, and smart phones. Information is much more mobile now; it can travel much more quickly and through many different types of devices. Instead of newspaper ads, window signs, or word of mouth, the Internet is the primary source for job listings and search tools. You can get news of job opportunities nearly anywhere in the world.

Public libraries carry books and periodicals that can assist you in virtually all phases of your job search including resume and interview preparation; they can even provide questions for you to ask during an interview. Resources can tell you how to prepare for the interview, how to dress, how to negotiate your offer, and anything else you need to know. This is good news, because it has increased the avenues by which you find out about jobs and how to prepare yourself. If there is a downside, for some who are not familiar with this practice, it is that it requires you to change how you make contact with a potential employer.

Often times, people ask me about the influence of social media on the role of Human Resources and more specifically, on the job search process. While most of these people have accounts with various online groups, they don't typically think of or utilize these sites in terms of job search, but rather to build their social networks. Many, in fact, don't even utilize these sites while they are employed to build professional networks that can now or in the future be used to assist them in their job search efforts. These sites can in fact play a large role in this effort and I'd suggest you have these accounts (I'm not a proponent that you do this during work hours) and keep it updated. This will be discussed again in the branding portion of this book.

Common practice dictates that you will need to expand your job search to view company websites as it is common practice now for company websites to list their available job openings. You can use the larger social media networking outlets such as Facebook, Twitter, LinkedIn and many others, to make connections with people for the purpose of obtaining a new job. You establish how much information can be viewed by others, such as the business you're in and your skills and capabilities; you can display them worldwide or to a selected group of members, both known and unknown to you. Company recruiters often use these sites to solicit job candidates; however, as always, referrals continue to be far and away the best source for new positions.

On these sites you can also find groups of members including groups for fellow job seekers, and connections to specific employers. There might be veterans groups or groups of school alumni, groups for school majors (like business administration, electrical engineering, etc.), and support groups. Seek all opportunities to participate in group interaction where employers or other employed members interact with members.

While there are still the large Internet job board sites like CareerBuilder, Monster.com, Craigslist, Beyond.com, Employmentnetwork.net, jobs-to-careers.com, Ziprecruiter.com and Snagajob, where a variety of different jobs will be listed, you also need to become familiar with industry or job specific websites that seek specific talent. For example, DICE.com carries listings for technology jobs, while Callcenterjobs.com, is a search site for call center representative jobs. If you are not computer literate, you still have time to learn. If you don't own a computer, go to a public library to use one. You can find computer training at many local colleges, job placement centers, and trade schools and you can use the Internet resources in their computer labs. Explore government assistance programs like the Trade Adjustment Assistance Program , which assists those who have lost jobs due to foreign competition and the Workforce Investment Act Dislocated Worker Program, which is for those who have lost jobs for other economic reasons to see if you qualify.

The job search process is truly a job in itself at least until you learn the new basics. Sorting through all the information available can take many hours. You will be amazed at how much there is. Now, you could convince yourself that it's overwhelming, but you know what? It really isn't. Understanding and utilizing these tools is like building the foundation of a house you can rely upon for years to come.

Remember the Three Little Pigs? Two of the pigs' houses could not withstand the onslaught of the big bad wolf, but the third pig built a brick house that could. The job search process is not that different. Will yours be built of straw, sticks, or bricks? After all, in the end, all three houses have four walls and a roof. But I can assure you that there is a difference. What do you think it is?

Experience has taught me that what we get out of something depends on the effort we put into it. If a project lacks preparation, energy, and focus, then we're destined to repeat what we set out to do and simply not sell it as we intended to. In other words, the job you find (should you find one) will likely be beneath your skill level and will have little or no opportunity for advancement, the company will not be one of the better places that you work, and (as I know has been true for me) it won't be a long-lasting job, either. It simply will be a bad fit-"just a job" and a place to kill time".

Now, I did not write this book for that reader. The reader I want says, "I want my home and its four walls and roof to mean something". My job search methods have to stand on their own and not collapse my universe under the pressure of a bad economy [the wolf]. Each wall signifies a completed step in the job search process (resume/cover letter, interview skills preparation, brand/character building, and the job offer itself). With the four walls completed, add the roof, and you're on the company payroll. Now, even if economics comes along and takes this job away from you, through no fault of your own (perhaps you are the newest person on the payroll),you know that the skills and foundation that you've built will help you to find your next job. You can then say, "I know in my heart that my work performance was good, that I built a sound reputation every day and that my job loss was not because my contribution wasn't good enough".

Clearly, your effort and your plan require you to differentiate yourself from the others. If you don't have contacts within the company or having someone referring you for the job, there are only two ways to differentiate you from either the onslaught of resumes that the company will receive or in the candidates the company will interview:

- the quality and delivery of content in your resume
- the quality, preparation, and ultimately, the performance you display in your interview

Did I get your attention?

There are so many free learning tools out there on resumes that it simply did not make sense for me to show you another variation on resume layouts, whether to make it in a chronological or functional format, have varying font type styles, or even if it should be in different colors. Instead, regardless of the format you find works best to convey your skills and experience, the book's focus is on doing the research on companies, understanding what the company is seeking in its job candidates through analysis of the job advertisement, developing your resume to deliver content, the actual resume submittal, the preparation for and then doing the interview, and ultimately, getting a job.

You may, in fact, decide after reading this book that you want to utilize a particular resume format found on the Internet or even pay to have your resume designed for you (with your input because it is **YOU** that the resume is selling). While someone else may be more design creative than you and can help you to succinctly put the words to both style and print, it's your skills and experiences that are being conveyed to the reader. You need to own what's printed and be active in both the content and review of the resume that bears your name.

Whether you design your own resume or have someone do it for you, there are certain "givens" that any resume will have. Those "givens" are:

1) your name and contact information
2) your level of education
3) reference to your role, responsibilities, skills, job title, and employer's name
4) employment dates with that employer

5) reference to your role, responsibilities, skills, job title, and previous employer's name

6) employment dates with that employer

Now, depending on the resume format you select (chronological-driven by dates with most recent employment and employer first **OR** functional-resume designed around skills and experience), these "givens" will be shown to prospective employers, but they will be displayed differently.

Assuming we don't know the resume format the company would prefer to see in the resume (unless a specific resume style is requested in the actual job posting), I would encourage you to have your resume available in both formats, then answer these two questions before submitting one style over the other:

- which resume format best represents you based upon the information available regarding this particular job posting
- is this company most interested in your specific role and responsibilities or do you sense that they are looking for a specific level of responsibility with [a] particular employer or two or more employers

The chronological resume format is more likely to attract the reader looking for a specific employer, specific role, and dates of employment. Most employers will prefer the chronological formatted resume. The functional resume is addressed to attract the reader looking to see if you performed a specific type of work with less attention focused on the specific employer(s).

The bottom-line here is that you want to submit to the employer a resume that "speaks" to the job posting. What that means is that the resume content "speaks" to the words used in the job posting. The resume address the specific language placed in the job posting by repeating those same words within your resume. This way, you are readily prepared to share with a company a product (your finished resume) your potential employer will want to buy by offering you a job. Remember, for purposes of resume submittal, you do not send one of each resume format but rather pick one formatted style and send it. Again, the chronological formatted resume will be the one they are most familiar with but you will find some number of employers in specific industries that will prefer a functional resume. There is no hard and fast rule here. Most companies will expect resumes sent to them to be done so via email or through an online submission form.

Regardless of the resume format you choose, I want this thought engrained in your brain each and every time you communicate non-verbally (or verbally for that matter) to anyone that has influence over your ability to be hired-"You have about a minute and a half to two minutes tops"--- to get the reader's attention. If the recruiter or hiring manager cannot make heads or tails of your resume or cannot find meaningful words in it that specifically address the open position, your resume is simply not effective and won't get you through the lobby doors.

Did you know that well over 50 percent of all submitted resumes (whether read by a person or through an automated system) are estimated not to meet the basic requirements of the open job? That number of disqualified resumes grows when you have the basic requirements of the job posting but very simply cannot effectively communicate that you have those necessary skills. Don't find yourself in the bottom 50+ percent-put yourself in the top 50 percent pile.

Whether it is a recruiter or an automated process (known as an applicant tracking system) reviewing the numerous candidate submittals, they will most often sort through these submittals to quickly identify key words in your resume. That is why I want you to place so much emphasis upon key words in the development of your resume or on-line submission document. Simply get in the habit of identifying the key words within a job posting, put those within your resume, and utilize them to effectively inform and attract the reader to both read your resume submittal and get you interviewed. For purposes of submittal, I'd avoid sending any resume greater than three (3) pages (experienced applicants should certainly have a resume of 2-3 pages) unless the employer specifically calls out to applicants that you detail all of your experience and you cannot provide that experience in a shorter length resume.

Use a dictionary, thesaurus, and even the advertisements themselves to find words that will trigger the interest of the reader (recruiter and hiring person). In your resume, use the same words you find in the ad to describe how you accomplish your work. The bottom line is that, within a two minute window you have to sell the reader on your ability to learn the company and perform the job. Re-submittals are usually rejected by these systems so you must strive to make the first submittal one your best. Applicant tracking systems typically seek keywords (usually those found in the job posting), your former employers' names, the length of your applicable work experience, and sometimes, even the school(s) you attended.

As this economy has evolved, the employer marketplace has gone through an equal amount of change. Many articles about the job market insist that the resume as we know it today is on its deathbed. Whether it is or it isn't, there will always be some kind of tool, application or mechanism for delivering your message to a prospective employer. The content of a resume, no matter the format, will continue to be every employer's means to evaluate you as a prospective employee.

Believe it or not, I'm convinced that the job search process is a science-therefore, it requires substance and attention to detail. If your resume lacks that attention and level of detail regarding your skills/experience, you likely will be passed over by another applicant who more clearly details their skills/experience. Employers clearly want to know you can perform the job.

I'd strongly suggest that you set up a filing system by company to track which version of your resume a company has. Keep the system in place until sometime after your job search is complete and you are satisfied in the new job.

Although I have not yet seen much in the way of published data on how effective it is, some job applicants are now including "quick response codes" (QR codes) which actually appear on their resumes. A recruiter or hiring manager can then scan this QR coded resume with a smartphone and it will actually connect them to an Internet link, such as to a candidate's personal website, presentation, or their portfolio. Applicants can therefore submit enhanced information to potential employers on an ad hoc basis to further support their job candidacy.

Specific as to how to show education on a resume, I'd suggest you give this some thought. If your education is your major selling point, it should be listed closer to the top of the resume and ahead of the experience. New college graduates or re-educated persons who want to highlight their new learning rather than their previous work experience would do this. When your experience and specific job knowledge is more important than education from years ago, list the work experience first. The resume and cover letter should both emphasize what you are "selling" and want the reader to be most interested in.

The expression, "it's all in the delivery" is exactly what these two documents need to do for you.

While I will give some examples of resume formats, my point isn't to challenge or change the format you're using. I just want you to use a format to greater success than many people do. There are numerous books and websites out there that will tell you something about resume format and content. You simply want to design a message that both demonstrates and communicates your experience and abilities in a style and with word choice that captures the reader's attention.

Now, Scott will take a recent job posting and create two distinctly different looking resumes (one chronological and the other functional) to demonstrate the difference in styles here.

Here is the job posting Scott will be responding to:

Senior Customer Service Rep

Seeking an experienced senior level customer service representative for our world class fishing resort located just outside the city limits of Sitka. Catering to fishermen from throughout the world, the position will encompass significant customer contact, both phone and clerical support, scheduling, cashiering and may include tasks such as general housekeeping duties when called upon. This is a multi-tasked, full-time, hourly compensated role so flexibility in scheduling is required. We seek experienced individuals who have worked in a customer service environment who can multi-task and demonstrate a customer service can-do attitude. Submit your resume in confidence to: Great Neck Fishing Lodge, P.O. Box 5678, Sitka, AK 99835. No phone calls please.

A critical element to any job search is to interpret the information provided to you by the job posting itself. The questions to be answered include: any and all key words that speak to requirements, i.e., soft (non-technical such as communication, temperament, style) and hard (technical such as system, process, computer, office, and years of experience) skills. Often times, knowledge of a particular industry can be particularly beneficial to a potential employer. Our understanding this information can then help us to shape our cover letter and resume response to this specific job posting. We clearly want to convey to this employer that we clearly meet the posting requirements and are in fact, the person to fill this position.

Now what did and did not appear in the advertisement?

The key words identified in this posting are: experienced, senior, significant customer contact, multi-task and flexibility. Let's now incorporate those words and repeat them either directly or indirectly using words of similar meaning in our resume submittal to the company.

Here is an example of a chronological resume you could submit for this role:

Scott Gardner
123 ABC Drive, Sitka, Alaska 99835
(907) 123-4567, ScottGJS13@gmail.com

Objective: A lead or senior level customer support role with Great Neck Fishing Lodge that will allow me to utilize skills that my previous employer recognized as attributes. Skills include: quality customer service and effective team player with excellent knowledge of company products and services. My employers have received numerous customer appreciation letters complimenting my efforts.

Experience:

Joe's Travel Service, Sitka, Alaska (2004-2012)

Clerical Support Representative

In this multi-functional role, I handled all customer inquiries including billing for this locally-based travel service that matches customers with various lodges, motels, and travel sites within the State of Alaska. Position required that I effectively communicate through various communication tools the various services and support available to the business's customers. Assigned to work with all customers in problem resolution, I followed up with all service requests, billing and collections questions, and all issues of relevance to both employer and customer. Interfaced daily with customers, management and the various functions within the office.

Key Accomplishments:

- Managed a high-volume workload within a deadline-driven environment.
- Exceeded expectations in all performance reviews scoring highest in communication skills, listening skills and meeting/exceeding the customers' expectations.
- Completed an outside voluntary customer service training course to learn ways to enhance customer satisfaction and improve productivity.

Personal Interests:

Actively involved in numerous local community efforts including Red Cross, American Cancer Society, Alaska Raptor Research Center

Education:

General Educational Development Diploma (Due 12/2013)

Now, let's walk through both the posting and the resume [Scott] developed and submitted for this job posting.

The posting called for an experienced customer service rep. While Scott's direct title did not show customer service in the title, Scott did reference the word," customer", numerous times in his resume including it in both the objective and in the work experience sections of his resume. He also showed he had been with this employer for eight (8) years so that should qualify him for both an experienced and senior level role. Scott was also quick to point out in both the objective and in his experience the recognition he has received from customers for his excellent customer service. This would certainly be attractive to many employers. His use of the term, "multi-functional", also demonstrates Scott's experience in working in different (showing flexibility) capacities while retaining the one job role and title.

Because Scott's education may be viewed as detrimental to his job search efforts, he placed little emphasis on his current level of education by placing it at the bottom of his resume. There was no education requirement stated in the job posting. The planned approach here was to focus on skills and experience rather than education. By placing the employer near the top and explaining the travel service business, Scott is able to connect the lodge and the travel business to both the travel and services industries. The emphasis on volunteer work is there to show a continued willingness to both help others and support a cause of interest to the local community (outside of work). When placing personal interests on your resume, be both cautious and conservative in your approach so as not to offend any resume readers who may not share your religious, cultural, or political beliefs. I have often discouraged applicants from putting any personal interests on their resume and leave that as an open topic to be discussed in an interview with a potential employer should the employers initiate the subject.

Again, the resume did not lose focus on the key requirements, elements, and words displayed in this job posting. Where possible, the resume repeated words found within the job posting and focused on the candidate's ability to gain recognition from his customers for his outstanding customer service skills while downplaying the candidate's (less than high school) education.

Now, here is Scott's functional styled resume responding to the same advertisement:

Scott Gardner
123 ABC Drive, Sitka, Alaska 99835
(907) 123-4567, ScottGJS13@gmail.com

Objective

Customer service position with Great Neck Lodge that will parlay 8 years of demonstrated organizational, customer service, and support experience.

Profile

Highly driven, customer focused employee who thrives on meeting and exceeding customers' expectations. Quick learner, company loyal, focused on the customer experience, diplomatic and tactful in communications. Proven ability to multi-task and be role flexible in a busy work environment that is deadline-driven.

Skills Summary

- General and Front office Skills
- Computer Literate
- Customer Service
- Scheduling and Billing
- Provide all levels of correspondence

Professional Experience

- **Customer Service**
- Handled all customer inquiries including billing for this locally-based travel service that matches customers with various lodges, motels, and travel sites within the State of Alaska.
- **Communications**
- Effectively communicated through various communication tools the various services and support available to the business's customers.
- Assigned to work with all customers in problem resolution
- Followed up with all service requests, billing questions, and all issues of relevance to both employer and customer.

- Interfaced daily with customers, management and across departments

Key Accomplishments:

- Managed a high-volume workload within a deadline-driven environment.
- Exceeded expectations in all performance reviews scoring highest in communication skills, listening skills and meeting/exceeding the customers' expectations.
- Completed an outside voluntary customer service training course to learn ways to enhance customer satisfaction and improve productivity.
- Received numerous letters from customers recognizing outstanding customer service

Employment History

Joe's Travel Service, Sitka, Alaska

Clerical Support Representative (2004-2012)

Education

General Education Development Diploma (Due 12/2013)

In this example, Scott is clearly first emphasizing skills and experience rather than focusing attention on the employer. Again, as in the first resume, you see little emphasis placed on his level of education. The hope here is that the tasks and projects performed will attract the reader looking for a specific skill-set in the position.

As you can see, both formats address the job posting using specific language. Look at both, decide which to submit for this particular opening, and move your attention to creating the cover letter to be attached to it.

On the subject of cover letters, I am a proponent for submitting them with the resume. They are simply a support document that supports the resume attached to it as they often summarize in a few paragraphs the experience being shown on the resume. It's also another document that has both my name and contact information on it while allowing me another opportunity to be in front of the person who is likely deciding who will be interviewed for the open position.

They can be as short as 2-3 paragraphs but are typically no more than three-quarters (3/4) of a page. Here's a sample in response to the job posting at the Great Neck Lodge:

Scott Gardner
123 ABC Drive
Sitka, Alaska 99835
(907) 123-4567, Email: ScottGJS13@gmail.com

April 18, 2013
Great Neck Fishing Lodge
P.O. Box 5678
Sitka, AK 99835
Attn: Hiring Authority

In response to your recent job posting for a Senior Customer Service Representative, I respectfully submit my resume for your consideration. I ask you to please consider the following:

- My eight (8) years of employer loyalty and customer recognized experience in the travel services industry.
- My demonstrated willingness and ability to multi-task to meet the demands of both business and customer

I welcome the opportunity to interview with you about this important position. My resume is attached.

I may be reached by phone or email and would welcome the opportunity to meet with you to discuss how I can contribute to the growth of your company and add to your customers' travel experience.

Sincerely,

Scott Gardner

Now, letters such as what you see here do not need to be either elaborate, or long. They simply are another tool from your toolbox that you, the job applicant, can use to show a potential employer the importance of good communication. It is also a tool, if separated from the resume, that can bring the employer back to your skills, experience and contact information and that's what you want. You want this employer to reach out to you for an interview.

Always remember that the purpose of any document you give to a potential employer (whether it is a resume, a cover letter, a letter of introduction, or something else) is to sell you. If a document doesn't prompt the reader to want to speak to you, it needs improvement. Bottom-line, you want to intrigue the recipient to want to know more about you. Be creative but accurate in describing who you are and what you offer. Employers are not just looking for who you are today; they are considering the future benefit of employing you tomorrow.

Be excited that you have complete power over how to describe yourself. Don't hesitate to seek help if you simply cannot find the words that help explain who you are. Never forget though, that the document must be accurate and that in an interview, you will have to explain what you have written in the resume and how you can clearly benefit your future employer.

CHAPTER 6:
Approach To Job Search

While your particular job search effort may not be global in nature, you need to remind yourself that many companies are in fact doing business globally (what is often called global expansion) and search globally to hire people (termed global recruiting strategy) to fill their jobs. So, your job search strategy and approach to the job search process most certainly needs to expand to include all international companies recruiting here to fill their open jobs. In fact, their hiring here is much more prevalent than many people think.

As both large and small companies have explored ways to sell their products and services to a more competitive, global marketplace, more of them have questioned the mindset that a product has to be developed and provided by United States based employees (many countries throughout the world, including the United States are seeing this). They asked themselves if they had the resources, processes and capabilities to manage a lower-cost workforce in different locales and get the same, or better, results. Now, we all know this but we need to remind ourselves that companies are simply looking under every rock (throughout the world-not just in the United States) to keep total business operating costs down. While selling to a worldwide market AND using labor sources located throughout the world, companies can often afford to offer lower salaries, because they now have significantly more candidates for any open position. Since the cost of labor is still significant for nearly all companies, many are not only reducing headcount, but are also scaling their technology to reduce operation costs.

This is different from what happened in our parents' generation. Then, layoffs and cutbacks were avoided until absolutely necessary. Companies showed incredible loyalty to their employees; in fact, employee layoffs were often never considered in business decisions. Similarly, expansion was often done in the same location or in a neighboring community. Employee referrals were the main method of recruitment so family members or friends joined the same companies. If a local community was determined unsuitable for expansion, the company chose another, but within the United States.

Today, many companies acknowledge that their talent pool is worldwide and that worksites can be in many countries throughout the world. What were once considered traditionally based U.S. Companies with U.S. based employees, now look at India, for example, and continue to make significant investments in people skilled there in soft and hardware engineering, as well as in call centers. In fact, U.S. companies now scour the globe in search of lower-cost workers, staffing call centers in the Philippines and Latin America too, while then expanding production and assembly facilities in Taiwan. Most importantly, they look beyond the United States for professional, scientific, and engineering talent and given the reduced work visa quotas established by the United States Government, these companies have gone so far as to set up local offices or workstations in other countries to meet their talent needs.

None of this is new news as companies have openly communicated these policies, much to the chagrin and dismay to U.S. workers. Many job opportunities once sought in the U.S are clearly no longer available. Workers throughout the world have been shaken by this change in business philosophy and that has created great mistrust between employee and employer never seen before. In many companies, employees' loyalty to their employers regardless of the company's past has been shaken by these kinds of business decisions. We have all had to learn that a global recruiting strategy may eventually impact our own jobs and careers.

Clearly this new economic environment (which began to take shape in 2008), has created a new work climate for workers worldwide. The good news is that there are still a significant number of companies (both large and small) and open jobs available to those whose skills and experience stay current, while they remain flexible in work location, employer, and salary.

Do I think that the pendulum has swung clearly in favor of the employer? Given the large number of applicants for most open positions, the pendulum seems to have swung heavily in favor of the employer. Does that mean that the employer now dictates all terms of the employment relationship? In most cases, Yes, but very talented individuals with the right kind of skills and experience can still negotiate the most the competitive market will pay.

Many companies looking to grow haven't changed their strategy that they will invest in recruiting the best and brightest. What I do see though is that salaries and benefits today will only be as competitive as necessary to out-recruit the competition and not as generous as in the past.

While most people find a new or changing marketplace for their talents and abilities for what looks like some time into the future, people are also seeing roles and responsibilities expanding (usually as a result of job consolidation), and total pay equal to or less than what they might have been paid in previous role changes. Evidence clearly shows that many looking for work simply struggle to find a total employment package equivalent to what they have made in the past. It is very clearly a changed marketplace. In tune with that, many companies you hear about report fewer advancement opportunities and lower merit increase budgets.

You may or may not agree with me about what this all means in your job search. While we all can agree that some opportunities have disappeared for now (or forever, in some cases), we cannot allow any company's global recruiting strategy to impact the focus we need to demonstrate in our job search efforts and more specifically, in our efforts to get hired.

Here's something that may help you to understand this changing marketplace. All too many times in my recruiting career, I've seen jobs small and large in number "reappear" in the local marketplace. Driven by various cost, quality and efficiency models, many industrial companies are continually rethinking their global expansion strategy. We see some of this happening today in some areas within the United States, specifically in manufacturing and production. While that field may not be your area of expertise, I believe it offers an instructive example of how the job market can change. Now, that is not to say that the job content or the skills required to do the job may not have changed at some level and that is what I believe you are seeing in certain manufacturing jobs where companies are struggling to fill these positions. In some cases, the jobs didn't change significantly but the people moved on. There are often times numerous reasons for these jobs not being filled.

Driven by various cost, quality and efficiency models, many industrial companies are re-thinking their global expansion strategy. You may see, in the near term, more and more manufacturing make a comeback in the United States. Recently, companies have expressed a need for people with specific manufacturing experience and are struggling to fill these positions in the United States. These jobs were once commonplace, but no longer are. Some companies have added additional skill requirements to these positions.

Why were these jobs lost, and where did the people who could do them go? There may be a few answers:

- When global expansion moved many of these jobs overseas, local skilled workers left for any and all opportunities in other areas of the country.
- Qualified (but unemployed) workers didn't go anywhere (letting their skills diminish) because they were tied down to a home that wouldn't sell and/or they were then or are now unwilling to leave loved ones to relocate short or long distances to fill these jobs.
- These workers changed careers (or retired) when their previous work left them dead-ended or unemployed.

What makes this all the more interesting is that unfortunately we are seeing in many areas of the country many who once performed jobs requiring a significant number of these skills now deemed by employers to be no longer qualified. Either time or circumstance has now passed them by-their skills no longer up to date, and some of those same companies they worked for no longer willing to re-train them- or anyone else. Rather, companies allow these positions to go unfilled while seeking the "perfect" hire. In fact, many positions open today have been open longer than it would take for those same companies to train less qualified, or even the person previously employed in the role, the "new" skills.

I'm also hearing that some number of companies don't want to invest in the training of this new talent pool; they would rather save their diminishing budget training dollars for their current, "performing" employees, but not always in the areas of greatest need. Until companies become desperate to fill some of these "key" jobs the problem will continue. Eventually, the company may invest in recruiting, change the job description and hire a "less or differently skilled" person. Or, the company will train a current employee to backfill the lower-level position, cancel the open position all-together, or may even slow or re-design the manufacturing plan in the hope that a suitable hire appears in the future.

Regardless of the reason or reasons as to why these positions go unfilled, as a job applicant interested in being hired for this "difficult to fill" position, you need to assess what a company's recruiting strategy is to fill this position and possibly determine your course of action to get hired for this job. Or, for the next one that comes along.

In this particular example, I would encourage you if you cannot develop a rapport with someone within the company that understands its business plan relative to hiring, to then reach out to local trade schools to see if this company is seeking to fill this position through them. If so, find out if this is one position or do they intend to hire more of these skilled people over some period of time. What recruiting sources are they using and develop a strategy as to how to gain the specific skills they seek through these same sources so that the company becomes interested in you. Ask yourself, what other contacts do I need to establish to build my network of contacts for this type of role now or in the future (don't forget: the course instructor might become a reference for you at some point)?

You simply cannot let an open position get past you. Create an action plan for getting you hired.

Here is an analogy that might help you visualize how getting a job plan going might result in you being hired:

Imagine you are a thoroughbred horse preparing to race. As you grow, you are likely to be imparted a method of learning and gaining knowledge in some way by those around you. As you mature and find a level of balance within your life, you know that training and preparation is essential to your overall success plan. As that young thoroughbred, you need to know how to enter a starting gate, how to break from the gate when the door opens, how to pick up your pace to stay even or better with competitors, and you need to have the endurance to finish the race. Your betting odds will be determined by people's faith in your ability to be first across the finish line.

Translated to the job search, this means you need to show through the resume and/or application process that the skills you've already obtained from schooling, work, and life experiences, plus those you appear capable of acquiring, make you a good bet to be a winning employee for them. You convey these things to a potential employer through a written document (resume and/or application) and through your ability to converse with them and sell yourself through an interview process.

For those people that have been unemployed for extended periods of time (either due to poorly managed job searches or to job skills that are no longer being sought by employers) or are looking to return to the workplace, there is more than sufficient evidence to show that your job search is much more of an uphill effort, but certainly possible. More specifically (and certainly within the current work environment), that is likely to mean that you will need to both expand the range of employers you will consider working for and submitting resumes to, while (if necessary) also lowering your sights on the open positions you will be willing to consider for employment opportunities. Your job search focus is on being interviewed and hired as soon as possible. Once hired, your plan is simply to improve your employment status with your new employer.

While you seek these new job opportunities, you should frequently review and improve upon your job search plan, strategy, goals and timetable. This includes taking steps to improve your skills training, job search network of contacts, and anything else within your job search plan and strategy that may increase your potential value to an employer. Start that today if you are just getting started.

CHAPTER 7:
What's Your Brand?

I describe brand as what people see or say about you (including your own personal level of charisma). It's more than just reputation. It's the way people react to you and to what they hear about you, and how they react when asked to comment about you. It has always been amazing to me how many employees I've worked with, or with candidates I've met, that do not know about the concept of brand, whether theirs is good or bad, or why they should even care about it. Others are totally shocked when they discover what their brand looks like, especially if it's one they do not believe fits them. In my experience, those people are the ones who ask why when they receive a termination notice, an interview regret letter, or receive no follow up at all following a 1st impression meeting. They get angry and lash out verbally at others for thinking bad things about them, and either close themselves off to the helpful approaches of others, seek others with similar or worse brands, quit the job or the job search, or stop being productive at all in other aspects of their lives.

Have you ever heard the expression that you were born with one mouth but have two ears? What do you think that says about each of us? To me it says perhaps we need to be better listeners before we become better talkers. Brand often times begins with listening. Frequently, the listening skills we use tell others more about our brand than anything we can or may say to them.

While it is important that you create a brand that projects your individuality and character, it is even more critical that your brand creation be what you want it to be. You not being conscious of your personal brand can put you into a deadly spiral in business, and in life, that is very difficult to overcome. Confusing people about who you are, what you stand for, and how you think does not build a convincing brand. Just like a bad experience of any kind, if your brand does not represent well who you are and what you stand for, people are not likely to return to learn more about you. Companies that don't learn this lesson fail. Those that don't meet (customer) expectations are no longer in business. By the same token, people who don't learn these life lessons are bound to repeat them, in one company after another, until their brand is so badly thought of that they simply cannot find anyone to hire them and they become underemployed or altogether unemployable.

Brand includes how you look, dress, speak, and how you conduct yourself with others. It includes your reputation-earned or not. Your brand can be formed early in any relationship; and in fact, lasting impressions can be formed as early as the first interaction or observance.

Before you solicit others to openly share with you what they see as your brand you should identify one term that you feel describes your brand. Do others share that same thought of you when you ask them what your brand is?

Brand speaks to what others know about you (beliefs, values, integrity, and character), your style (method of speaking/choice of words, how you conduct yourself in the presence of others, and how others perceive you) and your knowledge (job knowledge, areas of expertise, what you know).

When you are establishing your job search brand, it's important that you get to know and understand those around you-everyone with whom you come in contact or interact with. You need to be a person who believes that knowing something about someone makes you a better person, a more valued employee, and someone others rely on in making good business decisions. Even if you don't find redeeming value in someone beyond a one-time meeting, your knowledge and experience still benefits by the interaction. Knowledge combined with interaction is what builds your brand.

The importance of establishing your brand from the start of your job search cannot be underestimated. Brand-changing after the fact is extremely difficult to do when people already know you or know of you. Just think about those you know who have changed since you met. You can probably name them; often the change you've witnessed has touched you emotionally whether positively or negatively. Regardless of which, you remember their "first" brand, and it's likely your opinion of them has not changed (or at least, not dramatically). Visible repetition is the key to any effort towards brand change.

Now, change happens to us all, and for a variety of different reasons. In the workplace, it is often opportunity, or a lack there of, that creates a change (to whichever direction). When brand change is evident, it is witnessed by many more people than we think at a variety of different levels in the organization. If the change to our brand is drastic, the consequences can often lead to uncertainty or conflict. Such an example may be managing up in the organization as managing up in the organization is often where people tell me they have the most difficulty. This most often occurs when the person at the lower end of the hierarchy (most often you) does not have good and healthy communication with their direct management. What typically occurs next in this type of relationship (the relationship has stopped growing) is that there is a breakdown in trust. Managers that cannot trust and feel comfortable with their employees will often look to either compartmentalize that employee (place on specific projects of little meaning or projects that are heavily managed) or look to terminate the employee when the opportunity is there to do so. With either scenario, the person's brand can take a huge hit that may become irreparable with that employer (if you remain employed) or impact your job search efforts if not properly explained to a potential future employer (if given that opportunity).

To avoid being put into a position to mend such a relationship, I'd suggest you (the lower ended employee) take the necessary steps to both learn and accept the style of the manager (assuming the style does not violate legal standards) and work to build such a relationship. Most often that means completing projects that both compliment your individual and team work performance- AND -that of the work of your manager. It may also mean completing some portion of their (your boss's) work while taking no credit for it.

Now, constructive change such as that brought out by a good manager during a one-on-one project review or an annual performance appraisal, can be a career change catalyst for the employee who listens carefully to recommendations and understands the value of change. Without the belief that change can be good, our brands would never change or evolve for the better. But, all too often, someone who says he or she wants to improve brand takes what is said in these meetings as nothing but criticism. Countless times, I've listened to employees' brand concerns, but have seen them take no action to improve it. It is as if they believed that acknowledging the concern was in itself enough to change everyone else's opinion. (How could that be, if I'm the only one someone has told or acted it out to?) Do you know someone like that?

CHAPTER 8:
Linking Brand With Your Job Search

Throughout our careers, we run into those people in the workplace who truly don't know or seem to care what their brand is. They cruise the workplace like it's their property, like everyone is there at their calling, and that they have been gifted with more talent than they can find a use for. They come in and out of the workplace as if the doors fly open at the sound of their footsteps. Do you know one or more of these people?

I've come across more than a few. Often times they come with names or titles that they may or may not be aware of. Names like tyrant, a little Napoleon, conceited, self-consumed, or self-absorbed are some of the more common references I've heard.

Oftentimes, I was also the last person that spoke to them when the company and its management had had enough of them. In that parting moment, not only did most of these employees act shocked and overwhelmed at the thought of layoff or termination, but they were devastated at the idea that maybe their work ethic or level of productivity was not enough to keep them employed. Think they know what their brand is now (or what it was with that employer)?

Merriam-Webster's Dictionary defines brand as "a characteristic or distinctive kind" and "a class of goods identified by name". While I considered using the word, "reputation" here instead ("overall quality or character as seen or judged by people in general" or "recognition by other people of some characteristic or ability"), I felt that **brand** was a better way to invoke the people we are working to become rather than those we might be identified as today. While there are aspects of ourselves we are happy with and can live with today, it's the brand we want to build going forward with our new employer that we want to project in the job search process.

I see branding as a critical element of the job search process. It is reflected in the words in your cover letter, your resume, or in an application. I'd go so far as to say that branding is an outcome of how you speak in your initial phone screening or even in your very first contact with a company via phone, Internet, or mail when you inquire about an open position.

Each and every time you reach out to conduct your job search, you ask the receiver of your message to form a positive, appealing perception of you as a person and as an applicant. In essence, you are asking them to remember you as a positive brand every time you interact. Your brand has to be real and it has to be who you are. It's not just how you see or think of yourself but rather how everyone around you sees you as it speaks to your character, your treatment of others, what people see in you on the good and bad days, and most importantly, what people can expect from you by knowing you.

Here is an exercise that may help you to better understand what I mean by branding.

First, picture yourself as an HR recruiter at a company you are interested in working for. Now, imagine yourself holding a foot-tall stack of resumes with cover letters. The goal here is for you to identify the key skills and experiences you need to pull from each of the resumes received. From the information gathered and reviewed, you must sort them into numerous slots in a large box: either those labeled with manager's names, or one of the two larger slots on the bottom shelf marked: "Hold" and "No Interest". Your desk must be clear at the end of each business day.

So, you must:

- Open and read at least a portion of each and every resume in your stack

- Identify which manager slot should receive which resume, or place it in the Hold or No Interest slot
- Meet with each hiring manager to review and discuss the resumes (and letters) you have forwarded on to them. Often times in these meetings, you may also share with the manager the key points you've identified from each of the resumes and letters you've reviewed and passed on so that you may better contribute to the manager's effort to both identify and hire the best possible person for the open role in the company.
- Do all the above while you continue to perform other aspects of your job while continually being distracted during this task (by phone calls, responding to e-mail, and speaking to each and every person who approaches your workspace)

Ultimately, your performance in this recruiter role is then measured by your ability to find each of these managers the best possible candidates for each of their openings in a specific timeframe. This effort includes making contact with each and every applicant whose letter you opened and put in a manager's box. Often, it also means that you are responsible for making the initial assessment of candidates' resumes, speaking with them by phone and sharing pertinent information with the hiring manager. Since you work closely with the hiring manager, your careful assessments take time and require you to quickly identify the key attributes of the candidates based on the information available.

Now, switch roles. You're the applicant now. What is your goal? Its:

- To avoid having your resume and letter placed in the Hold or No Interest mail slots
- To make sure that the HR recruiter places your submitted documents in the mail slot of the right hiring manager
- To do everything you can within the content of your resume and letter to get them read by the hiring manager and prompt him or her to offer you a phone screening and an interview

Now how do we do all that?

Imagine that your cover letter and resume is the preview of a coming attraction at a theatre. You need to sell the reader on the movie so that they want to see it. That is what a resume should be designed to achieve!

You want to get closer to the top of the screening pile, past the HR Recruiter (or automated applicant tracking system) and into the hiring manager's interview pile: you must establish the beginnings of a brand that attracts both of them. You must provide enough detail in your document that makes them want to know more about you. Whether live person or an automated system, the initial screening process follows a set of parameters (these can be rules, guidelines, key words, etc.) for picking out good candidates from the pile. Remember, you're just a document until it means something to the recruiter and hiring manager. The resume and cover letter are like a brochure for you. They are short brand-building tools that speak about you in your absence.

Solid resumes and cover letters are brand elements critical to your search. Do not underestimate the effort needed to make them work for you. A scrambled, unorganized resume with thin or poorly explained content tends too often to reflect poorly on candidates, especially if it doesn't link itself (its content) to the job opening. Poor branding means your resume ends up in the No Interest slot. Truthfully, if you don't make the commitment to prepare your document properly, you shouldn't submit it. To do so might even eliminate you for consideration--for this or any other open position within a company. However, sometimes I received a well-written resume that was not suitable for a specific opening, but retained it in my hold file for days, weeks, or even a month or more for what I thought might be a more appropriate position. Commit to making every resume submittal the best it can be.

Let's say that your finished document (be it a curriculum vitae, resume and cover letter, application, or introductory letter) has now gotten you an initial meeting with a recruiter, HR rep or hiring manager. You now need to begin the psychological process of preparing yourself for this meeting. "Prepare, you ask?" " Why? I got the interview, didn't I?"

What if the recruiter tells you, "You are one of fifteen candidates we are considering for this opening"? What if you hear "We don't have an opening right now, but we are anticipating one in the next few weeks, (or months)"? What if you found out that "This is a team interview and, you will meet with the recruiter, the manager and two lead employees in a small conference room"? "What if the interview is three hours long with no break for lunch and you are told that if all goes well you'll meet with the department director or vice president the next day?" Are you physically and mentally prepared to "display your brand" when you arrive TOMORROW?

Job preparation is a science that requires significant time and effort. It is not simply creating a one, two or three page document that outlines who you are and the experience you have. It is about establishing a "-BRAND-" that speaks to people about who and where you are in your development as a person. An interview is almost like a movie's opening night or a TV pilot. Your initial screening can be like a show nobody wants to watch another episode of, or a series people want to watch. Your role as the lead actor means that people will be evaluating you from various vantage points and testing your demeanor, skills and experience to determine your "fit" with the company's and the team's culture.

Your branding effort should encompass every aspect of human behavior, because the details are what differentiate you from others. Otherwise, you are nothing more than "a face in the crowd".

Please read and understand this statement (written earlier in this book) again. These days, many jobs are open to anyone (and often anywhere) in the world. The global marketplace is not just for products and services; it is also for talent. Many larger US companies have operations throughout the globe and seek talent worldwide; some even allow employees to work remotely. This business and recruiting strategy allows employers to expand their access to top talent anywhere. The worldwide economic downturn has prompted global companies to significantly reduce the number of their jobs, pay levels, and locations. Many Americans continue to struggle with the significance of these changes and how their jobs and their futures are impacted. Expanding the global reach of products while controlling labor costs (which can often be about 60 percent of their total costs) is virtually all companies seek.

With nearly every open position requisition that comes across management's desk, companies around the world discuss controlling growth, managing costs, and more specifically, controlling the cost of human capital. Each new position is scrutinized for how its required skills, qualifications, pay, work locale, and reporting relationship fit into a company's cost structure. Getting approval to add employees has never been more difficult, in my opinion. My belief is that the hiring process will continue to tighten and that today's lower volume of jobs will remain steady or shrink until such time as companies feel they can increase their investment in their businesses. Therefore, my message to you is that you need to put in every ounce of energy you can muster to be the best candidate possible when a suitable position becomes available. You can go about achieving that by branding yourself as someone a company needs to continue its growth.

CHAPTER 9:
Submitting Your Resume

We all know that in today's job market, people get interviews for a limited number of reasons. The most common are: the person was referred; the resume was well constructed and showed promising current skills, experience and future capabilities; the person had specific credentials, licenses, and certifications sought by employers. Hearing of employers' interest is the logical step between submitting your resume and before the interview phase.

If your resume is attracting attention, you are obviously ahead of those who are getting little to no feedback after several submissions. Most likely, a lack of feedback (assuming you have followed the plan and strategy outlined for you in this book) means you are applying for positions outside the scope of what a company thinks you are capable of today, there are no such opportunities with that employer, or possibly your brand is known to someone in the organization but is not well regarded. If there are no appropriate opportunities, that is one thing, but if you are not being interviewed for bonafide openings, then you need to delve deeper into why you are not being considered. Since it is highly unlikely that the employer will tell you why you are not a clear candidate, you must rely on other information to determine why, so that you can develop a strategy that improves your chances for an interview.

First, examine the experience required of the candidates in the job posting. Do you truly have that level of experience, and is it clearly stated on your resume? If qualified, you need to re-work your resume. Are you using the right words taken from the ad to clearly state what skills and experience you bring? Now, having done that, is it clear to the reader or system that you clearly have the necessary skills to perform the role? It is in these times, you have to ask yourself why you submitted a resume that was not your best effort and make the decision as to whether or not to re-apply. If not qualified, you should move on to the next prospective employer from your research.

In todays job market it is not uncommon for the prospective employer to request a salary history, salary requirements, or both as part of the job posting process. The most common reason for the request goes back to what was discussed earlier. Job postings are the result of an approved job requisition process that included gaining budget approval. Budget approval implies that a specific amount of dollars will be paid for this open position and that the position will be filled at a particular time within the budget year. Hiring someone outside (over) the range of this budgeted dollar amount is likely not to be approved so hiring managers look to fill their open positions at or below the budgeted dollar amount. So, the request for salary information from prospective hires can then be used as an additional screening tool by the hiring manager to assist her/him in their hiring effort. Now, candidates can be screened by recruiters and hiring managers based on resume and salary history/requirements.

When salary history and/or requirements are required as part of the posting process, it's best not to ignore the request to provide them. Many companies will choose not to review candidate resumes where salary history and/or requirements are not provided. Simply put, do not submit resumes without this information if you expect your resume to be taken seriously. While there is always that very slim chance that your resume may "slip by", it's more likely to go in the "No Interest" pile and your effort and the opportunity to be considered for the open position will then go bye-bye.

While you cannot change your salary history, you certainly can word salary requirements back to an employer that the employer may consider. Typically, you want to leave the salary requirements discussion open until such time as the interview process is either well underway or even better, you are at the salary negotiation phase. Always best to avoid salary discussions early in what I'll call "the courting or dating phase", when both you and the employer are getting to know each other. Strategically, this may be the best time for you to know how potentially valuable you are to the employer and what you can reasonably expect in an offer from that employer.

If the employer requests salary requirements as part of the resume submittal process, you may be best suited to try and locate salary data via the Internet for similar roles in the same geographical region as the open position and use that data in your submittal.

The interview, if there is one, often goes to someone who projects his or her brand better on paper than you. Nowadays, companies just don't hire if they cannot get someone with all the skills and experience they seek. Even the best qualified candidate will not be hired if he or she is missing anything or is outside the hiring range for the opening. This can lead to fewer candidate interviews and fewer hires.

If you don't have the specific skills sought, can you obtain them? Can you get additional education (and can you pay for it)? What skills have you marketed in the past and where have they gone?

A specific course certificate may make you more employable, and it may be your best choice. If the lack of a certification or two is preventing you from getting interviewed, then develop a strategic and financial plan to get what you need. Just be sure that you really need it: thoroughly research and confirm it. Decisions without research are often bad and can have dire financial consequences. Specialized education is only valuable if there are employers that value it.

It is very common for company management to solicit the opinions of respected employees about applicants. If someone in a company knows you, it is a clear example of how your brand can follow you along your career path. (It does happen; don't be naïve). Opinions like these can have a significant impact on whether or not a company interviews a candidate who appears to meet the qualifications. If you are turned down despite being a good match for the job on paper, then reestablishing your brand should be an essential element of your job search process. Begin that process immediately while soliciting employers that do not know you or, if need be, move to a new community and restart your career.

If you believe your brand is good, don't hesitate to build upon your personal network and politely ask them to be advocates for you in your job search. Although friends or former co-workers are not always aware of openings within their companies, they are often happy to put in a word for you when they hear of any. If you find out about an opening on your own, reaching out to someone whom you know in the company is often the best way to get introduced to those who can hire you. As the saying goes, "leave no stone unturned".

Many people have turned to social networking tools like Facebook, Twitter, LinkedIn and others to keep their names and faces in front of friends, past associates, and co-workers. The tools and methods you use to stay connected with others is certainly a personal choice but the message is clear; stay connected.

Social media has had an enormous impact on the world. It has created new companies, new ways to dispense information (good and bad), and new job opportunities, among other things. It also now influences how others e-view us positively or negatively. Such perceptions can be shared globally in a matter of seconds.

Companies use social media to see what others may be saying or hearing about them (this is called "buzz"). They also use these sites to solicit individuals with specific talent and to check on the behaviors and actions of their own employees. In other words, companies have hired and fired based on information from these sites.

Remember that companies and recruiters mine social media to learn about you; a negative online image can kill a potential job if you aren't careful. Always evaluate the possible consequences of your on-line presence in social media before (and during) employment. I could tell you stories about how some of the best and brightest were not hired, not promoted after being hired and even got fired because of their on-line presence. Regardless of your path, as a piece of advice, you need to be very, very careful about how you are or may be perceived in your job search.

Information on social media sites can therefore impact your brand in good and bad ways. As part of your overall job search strategy, always think about how you want to be viewed; -how you want your brand to appear to others-on social media, because it is very difficult to change your message once it has been out there for others to see.

CHAPTER 10:
Interview Preparation

Preparing for an interview means planning:

- how to look and what to wear
- where to go, when to be there, and how to get there
- the impact on your current schedule (and the schedule you are impacting)
- what you need to know about the role and the company

When preparing for an interview, you have the advantage of being able to study many documents well in advance: the content of your resume, the job posting itself, and documents about the company (such as annual reports, news articles and your own research on their products, services, culture, and management).

Over the years, even interview clothing has gone through major transitions. Men once wore a tie and slacks or even a suit; women wore a nice dress or pants suit. In some environments, that has changed dramatically. Don't make assumptions about what you should wear; ask your interviewer or the HR department what is appropriate. If you don't ask, I suggest you overdress rather than under-dress. Always arrive clean, with clean teeth or dentures, and never wear dirty clothes or have dirty hair. Try to preview how you look before you enter the building to make sure you look presentable. You might carry a small mirror or use your car mirror to check your teeth, corner of your lips, or eyes. (Never do this in view of others.)

Always plan to arrive at your interview early. Know your travel route, and don't hesitate to seek directions if you get yourself lost. Some people rehearse for the interview along the journey, while others prefer to simply focus on the commute and find a sense of calm. Do what feels best. If you have properly prepared and you project inner confidence, the process should flow smoothly. By the time you arrive at the interview, your image and brand should fall right into place. Always bring extra copies of your resume.

Your intention from the moment of your arrival at the company is to appear comfortable, confident, focused and ready to start work. From the moment you begin the walk to the front door, imagine your interview starting. Turn your phone off and put it away-this is an interview-a face to face discussion-use plenty of eye contact. Never walk in carrying a cup of coffee, tea, water, or an object you need to dispose of. If offered something to drink in a lobby, for example, only bring it in with you to the interview space if the interviewer suggests you do. Never have gum or candy in your mouth during an interview.

First and foremost, practice your presentation. Demonstrate how your background and skills is a great match to the new job's description. Repeat over and over in your head how you have used your developed skills to complete projects in a timely manner. Every company wants to hear how you are going to help complete projects on time and within budget, but in the interview give your examples concisely and without too much detail. Do not get wordy or talk excessively, or you risk losing the listener's attention. Interviewers are often more interested in structure and consistency of approach. For example, they want to hear whether a candidate has a process or personal formula for success, and to get an idea of how you get there as an individual and within a team environment. If you've received compliments from management or in previous performance reviews, you can mention them.

However, always be prepared to go into greater detail should you be asked; prepare both short and long versions. Always begin with the short one. Understand, too, that your interviewers will also examine the way you deliver your messages-your presentation style- to assess how you'll fit into the team. I've found that these moments put your brand well on its way to being established. Do not underestimate the preparation and effort required for this segment of the interview, as it often decides your suitability as a candidate.

In all my years as a recruiter and interviewer, I learned to avoid our natural tendency to form a perception of someone within the first two minutes. I still believe that people assess someone they just met in the first two minutes, and then spend the rest of the meeting trying to validate the opinion. This is not to say that opinions never change as discussion develops, but in general, an interview within a fixed length of time leaves little opportunity to change a bad start into a job offer. If an interviewer is inexperienced (perhaps a hiring manager), changes in the initial assessment seldom happen without discussion with others in the same interview team. Consider preparing and practicing for the two- minute drill and making a great first impression.

Once you feel comfortable about your message delivery style, focus attention on building a list of questions about the opportunity and the company. Have a few questions for each person that you may speak to. Here are some examples. You can use these or add to them:

- What attracted you to the company? How long have you worked here?
- What can you tell me about this position that is not referenced in the job description? (Have a hard copy of the posting in your hand when you ask.)
- Can you talk to me about the team that I'll be working with?
- How would you describe your leadership skills, and what are your expectations of me?
- What do I need to do to be successful in this role?
- What skills or attributes did you see in my resume that makes me a possible fit for this role?
- At what level may I be interacting with people in other departments?

Never downplay the prospective role or imply that it might be beneath your skills and abilities. You always have the option to turn it down if it is offered to you. Leave everyone wanting to hire you as this is likely to be where the best opportunities come from.

In a first interview, never ask questions about promotions, transfers, or other opportunities within the company. If there are aspects of the job you don't understand or want to know more about, carefully and safely phrase those questions so that they sound professional. If you have no questions about the role, ask questions about the company: "How would you describe the company culture?", "Who are your principal customers?", "What kind of communication does the department (or company) use (such as company meetings, e-mail, video conferencing, etc.)?" Ask the HR person about the salary range and benefits, when the position is available, the next step in the interview process, or when they anticipate a hiring decision will be made, and so on.

In your preparation for and then in your actual interview, you need to know and understand your audience and what role they play in the company. For example, do not ask an HR person about key aspects of the job, the team size, or what the department is working to develop. Ask those questions of the people within the department who interview you. If you don't understand a financial report, cannot learn to read one by your interview date, don't pretend to understand one when you interview. In addition to or as an alternative to the financial report, use any and all company documents available to you that will help you to understand its products and services, who it sells to, and which people hold positions of influence in the company. Knowing something about the company is essential to your preparation and presentation.

Last, you want the people of the company with whom you come in contact with to feel like they are members of an exclusive club that you want to join. You want to always leave your interviewers feeling that:

- you were prepared for the interview as demonstrated by your presentation, your focus and concentration, and use of effective listening skills
- you know about the company and are interested in what the company is doing
- after talking with everyone, you are even more interested in the opportunity than when you walked in

- you can be a valued contributor in the role, as part of the team, and working for the company

"Everyone likes me" is what you strive for here. Believe me, it will not always happen, and it may not need to happen in every interview, but it should be a goal you strive to achieve.

Preparing to interview for any role or job in today's marketplace is as important as anything you do when you wish to project a professional image. You set your sight on a role, make your best effort to get interviewed, prepare for the interview with every tool available, project confidence and comfort with yourself, knowing that you are fully prepared, and then give it your best effort. While we all hope to get everything we seek in life, including success in job interviews, some opportunities we won't be selected for. I'll leave it to a future chapter to discuss what you should do next when that happens. For now, let's focus on what you need to do to make the interview successful.

While what I'm about to say is important keep it in perspective. In recent years, most companies have altered their recruiting philosophies. Fewer job ads are being run, there are fewer staff people reviewing resumes; many companies only respond to those in whom they are interested, and many are expanding the administrative approval process for those they are considering for hire. Ultimately, this means that you may have a longer wait to receive a job offer, or you may never receive any acknowledgment for the effort you put in to prepare for and participate in your interview. While I think this is rude and unprofessional on the part of employers, it is, unfortunately, what many people experience during the search process.

You can be angry or frustrated with the job search process, and that is OK, but, it will not help you. You have to keep going and keep looking forward and minimize the amount of frustration you will allow yourself to show. Rather, look at it as if it is an obstacle course. To look at it any other way may seem overwhelming at times. When it feels overwhelming, stop, take a deep breath, and slowly inhale and exhale, over and over again, until you have a new plan of action. You have heard the expression that you can only control what you think and do, and that statement is true here, too. Your focus needs to be on continuing your job search and doing what you can to be the company's candidate of choice with every employer you come in contact with.

Professional behavior or courtesy does not end when the interview ends. Of course, you thank everyone at the close of an interview, but many people find that small, professional thank-you cards addressed and mailed to each interviewer a day or two afterward can be an effective tool in the job search process. It is simply another inexpensive way to keep your name in front of prospective employers in a tight job market.

Your card message can be as simple as the following:

Dear Ms. /Mr. X:

Thank you so much for meeting with me this past week to discuss the position of ____. I sincerely appreciate the time you spent and believe that my qualifications and experience are a great fit for this position. I believe I'd be a great addition to the team you are building, and would certainly look forward to the opportunity of working with and for you. You can reach me via phone or e-mail at _____ and _____.

I look forward to hearing about the next steps in XYZ Company's employment process.

Sincerely,

Your Name

CHAPTER 11:
Your Job Search Learnings

Whether your job search is the result of a job loss, the end of your military service, or graduation from college, trade school or high school, there are paths you can follow. Your future is not at a crossroads but rather on a detour. We all know about detours. A detour, as opposed to a road, is not necessarily a direct path. Life has many detours, and the "roadmaps" we have don't always tells us when new ones can show up. After all, maps are often drawn up after the roads are in place, not before.

Job search detours have increased threefold since the economic crisis of 2008, and few of us even have a clue when (or if) things might return to the way they were. Many roads have been damaged and possibly destroyed in the wake of this financial crisis. Given the extent of the financial damage, things might never be the way they were before.

We can choose to sit back and do nothing, or we can choose to do something.

We can:

- communicate with our elected leaders to encourage them to more effectively manage the dollars, programs and services under local, state and federal government control, rather than ignoring or just throwing our hands up at them

- both communicate and work with those leaders to encourage them to seek employers for our communities, so that they might bring facilities and jobs to the area
- take the time necessary to consult family and friends and make decisions around what is best for each of us going forward given the state of the economic climate
- Open our job search minds to employers of all sizes. Many of today's and tomorrow's jobs will be with small employers who will often pay less and offer fewer benefits

This book has provided you with some of the tools you need to begin the process of moving forward. Whichever path you follow, you have work experience and/or education to support you in your efforts to seek better employment. While the mechanics of your approach may be the same as those of many others, this book's roadmap contains numerous emotional and people sensitive steps and approaches that many others either neglect or choose not to incorporate into the job search process.

Yes, others will use some of the same tools and resources to locate job opportunities as you, but they likely won't have the knowledge or foresight to think about the importance of how a screener or interviewer reads a resume, or about what is required to get that attention. They won't know, even if they get the attention of the resume leader, how to get the best results in the interview process through active educated participation, presentation and questions.

You can also move a step forward as you learn and apply the process of branding yourself when you present "you" to a prospective employer. You not only can achieve the goal of being hired, but you can begin increasing your level of contribution and value to the company through your developing brand.

This book has focused on you and the steps you need to take to start, restart, or find who you need to be leading up to and in your return to the workplace. Many of us determine our self-worth by the jobs we have or don't have. I did the same for many years. That didn't change until I started to put all these thoughts in writing and read them back to myself.

While jobs don't make us who we are, I do believe that the value of our struggles and contributions as people can be found in the efforts we make every day. No matter how big, small, or repetitive a job is, it is our pride in how we perform combined with how we treat people all along the way that make us what we are. For it is the pride in what we do that carries over into our other life choices and into the friendships and family relationships we build along our journey. Building an unrivaled brand (one that genuinely speaks of us as individuals) for ourselves allows us, when we look forward and back on our lives, to know that we built something that will stay with us long after we have gone.

We discussed the importance of education and more importantly, the subject of ongoing learning. Learning is critical to each of us at every stage of our life regardless of age or condition.

We understand that personal choices have consequences, and that each and every major life choice has both short and potentially long-term effects on later decisions you'll want to make. We clearly need life choices to be thought through carefully.

We understand that documents such as resumes, cover letters, interview preparation notes, and thank you letters are the means of communicating our experience and skills in the best light to potential employers. Though companies may change the way they communicate their open positions to us, we know that the effort we take to put our best foot forward the first time is essential to our mission to be actively considered for each and every position we seek in the workplace.

We understand that as technology changes, the means by which we convey our message also changes. The content of the message may or may not change depending on the communications vehicle used.

We understand that people have points of view about each of us based upon their experiences with us. "Your brand" is no different from that of a soft drink, toothpaste, a shampoo, or soap. It's the finished product you represent to everyone you come in contact with. It can take only moments to develop and it can stay with us for as long as we know someone. It's a style; it's a persona that we project to others through our actions. It may be one that immediately attracts others to us, or it could be one that repels others. It could attract specific groups, specific individuals, or even no one at all. "Brand" is a critical component of a job search and it is just as important as any written document we create during the search process.

We understand too the importance and relevance of social media to the job search process today. While we may or may not participate on such sites, we understand that many people do use them actively to communicate with others. Whether we use the sites or not, we want any messages conveyed about us on them to be of a positive nature, since we know recruiters and others may seek information about us there.

Last, we understand that the loss of a job through layoff or consolidation may not be a direct reflection of our ability to perform a role, but may rather be a result of business, political, and economic factors we may not be able to control or change. We know that we can support our job search efforts with documentation such as performance appraisals, merit increases, job or role change notices, and so on that we can use to demonstrate our contributions on the job.

Never in my lifetime has the job search process been more time-consuming or difficult-but it is not without hope or opportunity. While I certainly cannot deny that the struggle going forward can be difficult and trying, there are new job opportunities developing every day. Certainly, they will most often be filled by the best-qualified or best-connected of candidates.

My dream was to have all my experience, and the preparation of putting this into print, connect with you. "Here is what I've learned from my years in human resources and in the business world. I hope you can successfully apply it to your job search efforts. I hope that what I have learned on my life journey has reached you early enough in your own journey that you have time to think through and make the decisions that are best for you and yours. After all, your journey is not just your own; if you are fortunate, it may have a great impact on the journey of others."

Thank you for allowing this part of me to be shared with you. I can be reached via e-mail at ScottGJS13@gmail.com should you wish to provide comments or ask questions.